Save Our Forests

by Rachel Russ

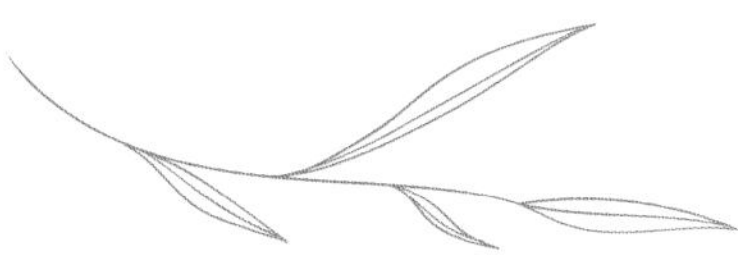

Mighty Forests

When you visit a forest, what can you hear? You could hear birds chirping and insects buzzing. You might even hear **mammals**.

Forests are full of life.

Sometimes, forests are cut down. Sometimes, they are lost in wildfires. Animals can be hurt or left homeless.

A bushfire smoulders.

Forests are important. Trees absorb gas. They clean the air.

Trees make a gas that humans need to live.

Tree roots drink up water when it rains. They help to keep soil stable.

Without trees, soil can be washed away.

Assam

In a place called Assam, people live and work along a big river. Over time, lots of trees were cut down.

After the trees were cut down, the soil washed away.

The **monsoon** came each year. It washed the river on to the land. There were no trees left to keep the soil stable.

Water washed away crops in the fields and destroyed homes.

Forest Man

A man called Jadav believed he could save crops and homes. He planted trees on the empty riverbank.

Jadav believed trees could help.

Jadav travelled every day to plant trees. The trees began to grow.

Jadav planted trees to save his home.

After a while, Jadav could use seeds from his trees. He tended to each **sapling**.

Jadav planted the seeds.

After many years, Jadav transformed the **barren** space. It became a massive, lush forest.

Jadav was given the name "Forest Man".

Animals Returned

The forest grew and grew. Jadav noticed lots of animals. They had started to come back.

Storks often roost in the trees.

Animals created a vibrant **ecosystem**. Tigers began to live in Jadav's forest.

Sometimes, elephants visit the forest.

Protecting the Forest

People wanted to cut trees for wood. Jadav helped people learn that the forest helps them.

Jadav faced many tests but he didn't give up. He plans to keep planting trees for his whole life.

Jadav's forest became a symbol of hope.

People Planting Trees

Luckily, Jadav is not the only one saving forests. People are planting trees all over the world.

There are lots of tree-planting stories.

When a boy called Felix was 9, he set up a group. He called it "Plant for the Planet". He aims to plant 150 trees for every person on Earth.

Felix plants trees with a friend.

Felix speaks at events across the world. He tells leaders to act.

Felix's group has gained interest from news channels.

Felix's dream inspires many people. Their collective effort has made a lot of progress.

Children planting trees.

Save Our Forests

In New South Wales, wildfires destroyed trees. The wildfires spread rapidly.

A lot of koalas lost their homes.

People are trying to revive the forests. They are planting trees for koalas. Koalas can live in them and eat the leaves.

We can protect koalas by planting trees.

Planting trees is important. Forests take a long time to grow. We also need to protect the forests we already have.

Some forests are very old.

Perhaps you could join a group to plant trees. This way you can help look after our planet! We need forests!

Glossary

barren: a place where no plants grow

ecosystem: a group of plants and animals that live in the same place

mammals: animals that have fur or hair

monsoon: a time of year when there are very heavy rains

sapling: a baby tree

Index